# Voice
## of a
# Wildfire

Never silence your voice!

*Jonine Jonis*

# Voice
## of a
# Wildfire

**Janine Tamis**

Janine Tamis
*Voice of a Wildfire*

The Self Publishing Agency
Copyright © 2020 by Janine Tamis
First Edition

Print ISBN: 978-1-7770635-0-4

*Cover and Book Design*  Laura Wrubleski
*Editors*  Kelsey Straight, Jessica O'Brien, Natalie Rae
*Publishing Support*  The Self Publishing Agency

*Dedicated to my Grandpa, and my Aunty Mary*
*You were the light of our lives—*
*a light that will shine on forever.*
*Rest In Peace*

CONL

*ents*

COU
AGE

R

*fear*

*I wish to be a wildfire,*
*but I'm too afraid to burn.*
*Here I am—*
*with embers in my hands,*
*writing about this passion*
*I have yet to light.*

We are living at
the edge of a storm,
never knowing when
it is about to break,
but always having
to be prepared for
the madness.

I live endless battles
within this steel cage
I call my soul.

*My spine has cracked
along ridges of
mountains
I've been too afraid
to climb.*

You shadow yourself
from the world—
a hidden tragedy,
for if you step out
of the darkness
you would shine
a thousand suns
into existence.

Sometimes I worry
that I am too much,
like an earthquake
whose aftershocks
you will continue
to feel.

I fear the heaviness
will crush me,
long before I ever learn
to let go of it.

I'm too afraid for the waves
to call my name, chaos has
interrupted my life before,
washing me out too far
to swim home to shore.

*My storms have given me much to fear and more to overcome.*

My silenced words are the ghosts
I could not let go.

Dark voices leave contours
along my mind, moving their way
throughout my entire body,
banging my insides trying to
rattle me into submission.

*Survival is a tactic*
*we learn in a world forcing*
*fear through our hearts,*
*covering us with darkness*
*too evil to name.*

Fear is like being underwater,
consumed whole,
blanketed by darkness—
the undercurrent grasping
at your foothold, sinking in
its infinite layers and depths.
Don't allow yourself
to give in and ingest fear;
you can't swallow the ocean
it just leaves an empty hole.

My fear eats me raw
it gnaws on my bones
leaving teeth marks
in the very marrow
of who I am.

Let your soul wander
to the edge of fear,
and freefall into
its madness.

I fear my storms,
not realizing they are
the most beautiful part of
what makes me human.

*I have learned to
dance with my fear,
it steps on my toes
but I don't let it
lead me.*

COURAGE

*I am a story*
*in the shape of a storm*
*about to break*

*o p e n.*

I am but a thousand
poems away from
revealing my soul
in its entirety.

Our world will expand
every time we allow
ourselves to explore.

Bravery is held within
the bones of ourselves,
our movement forward
keeps us alive.

*Free spirits dive
into vast oceans
finding home
in the beauty of
their depths.*

Be open to the universe
lying deep in your dreams,
don't let anyone tell you
it holds too much.
Your dreams are yours alone—
don't be afraid to
show your greatness.

Her heart has been given
paths full of thorns yet she
continues to tread slowly,
bleeding beautiful truths into
this world, and still remaining
whole on her own.

*Your wings,*
*oh how they fit*
*upon your back*
*resting weightless*
*until you need their*
*strength in flight.*

*She had a way about her—*
spitfire with spine of steel,
never backing down from
a challenge, and facing life
head on.

Only I can extract my wild
from the depths of darkness
and turn it into purpose.

You walked through fire
to become the fire, and it is
beautiful how you have learned
to embrace your flame, where
others have burned to ashes.

*I am taking back
this life I've lost
from a darkness
I haven't been
able to name.*

There is something beautiful
about the way you move forward in life—
even with the world on your back,
you never let it weigh you down.

Scream and storm
beautiful one, so your
silence will know sound
and what it feels like
to be powerful.

We are born as ships
with no sails,
we learn to navigate our oceans
like we do dreams.

You have a spark within you
that when lit will turn into a
wildfire of beautiful intentions,
so don't be afraid to share
your flame with the world
and burn on brave one.

*Like powerful waterfalls*
*we surged over our edges*
*into new beginnings.*

I threw courage into the air
and grew wings to follow it.

There is a shift inside your soul,
an echo of bravery, allowing you to
stand tall and embrace the change
you are about to take on.

Fear consumed her,
so she ran into the wild
to find where courage
was born.

I extract words from
every corner of my soul,
they are my courage—
my way out of this silence.

*Quiet warrior*
*don't lose who you are,*
*you have the ability*
*to move mountains*
*with your stillness.*

*L*

*sing*

# FAILING

*I fall so heavy*
*and so often,*
*I leave craters*
*in this earth*
*in the shape of*
*a human being*
*who is trying.*

It is often the
silent hearts
and soft petals
that fall heavy.

I am a mess of volcanic thoughts,
I erupt daily.

The people who matter
witness your storm,
and help pick up the pieces
long after it ravages
the depths of your soul.

*The stars in her eyes
collapsed, they don't
shine how they
used to anymore.*

Don't be afraid to
freefall into the open
skies of your existence,
it is where you will learn
to grow your wings.

My bones are heavy
with ashes of the fire
that burnt out inside of me.

I fall apart faster
than I can fall back
into place.
I am left walking
towards humanity
with pieces of myself
in my hands, learning
to ask for help.

*A fearless heart sinks into your depths to save you from yourself.*

Some days I have to
remind myself, that
it is okay to cry the
depths of my oceans
out onto the land
of my existence.

I cannot arrive at death
having shoved my voice
so far down my throat
it never sees the light of day.

*My oceans have depths
too deep to discover.*

Smoke sends us a thick
and heavy coating of reality
into what our lives would be like
if we happen to burn
the wrong fire inside of us.

We capsize in oceans
we aren't meant to sail through.

Self-love is a battle
many lose, and it hurts
to watch as they let go
of their shield and pierce
the sword they hold
into their own soul.

*I fall as the crack*
*from my heavy silence*
*splits my spine in two.*

We are all just
navigating life
with a compass
that doesn't work.

My body is a haven
for chaos—I spend nights
sifting through the mess
to find my breath.

I wish my mind had a door
so I could just EXIT
out of my thoughts
sometimes.

*You cannot smother*
*the flames of someone*
*who honors their truth*
*and burns above it.*

I fall deep into my rising.

Our ability to rise up
like the sun
after a night of darkness
proves just how resilient
the human spirit can be.

My wings give way, but
falling means finding strength
beyond fear and imperfection,
believing in the possibility
of my design.

*If you burn out;*
*rest, reignite, and rise*
*as the flame of fire*
*you long to be.*

Madness became my identity
and those who stayed to watch me
unravel into something beautiful,
are the only ones I'll ever need
in my life.

Her soul was fierce,
her heart was wild,
and every breath
she exhaled was fire
under the stars.

I create my own healing
with madness in my soul,
no matter how much someone
tries to break me down, I will
rise whole, *every...single...time.*

You taught me
the art of self-love
as to paint myself
beautifully on
the canvas of
my existence.

The night sky
is embedded in my soul,
I love beyond darkness,
embracing the light in
everything and everyone
I see.

I rise into a woman
with an upright spine,
my newly found voice
unapologetic with reason,
confidence and power.

We are souls that spark
on the world's breath,
igniting flames of
new beginnings.

*You will find me ascending mountains where my purpose meets the skyline.*

Be unafraid to fight fire with fists,
and raise hell in this world of ashes.

She is rising,
and oh how beautiful
her wings silhouette
against the sky.

Your spark is unique,
and only you can light
into whatever flame
you wish to become.

Lay your broken wings
down to rest, and soar
with the strength from
the skies you have already
mapped and conquered.

*Your wild is born
the moment you believe
that you were made for
far more than being
a tamed soul in a
routine world.*

I pour my soul
into oceans of others,
hoping to make waves
that change their course
into currents of beauty
and tides of worth.

We don't always
have to be moving
to show our growth,
even in stillness
we can bloom.

She will rise between
silence and sound,
where her voice was born
and soul was found.

resilience

# SCARS

*We learn to love through armored hearts.*

I am a hurricane
trapped inside
a fragile body,
I collapse during
high winds and
messy days.

I hope you can
abandon the idea,
that you are less
deserving of life,
or love, than anyone
else in this world.

Your existence is essential,
so please don't leave quite yet
beautiful soul, stay awhile longer
so we can show you a world
that hurts a little less.

Some days
I embody the moon,
other days the wolf.
Lately I am the howl
caught in the space
between the two.

Our wounds cannot heal
if we cannot admit to the
circumstances in which
made them bleed.

Our scars breathe
when we unveil them
in their truth and
not in shame.

Be gentle tending to yourself
in the moments you break,
you are an open wound
to the world and in need
of a little self-love and care.

From time to time,
we all crackle
against our own fire,
like enemies of the flame
dissolving into ashes.

*I pick my soul*
*off the ground*
*and place it gently*
*into my body*
*as if you didn't*
*just try to take*
*the best parts*
*of my existence.*

May flowers bloom from
the places in your soul
that are left feeling dirty
and silenced by the hands
of those who tried to bury you
with their crimes.

I am a broken vessel
cracked by my ability
to only love myself
in pieces.

There are scars buried deep
within your skin and soul that
remind you of your hardest nights,
so tread lightly through the pain
and remind yourself that you are
only human and those days
will soon pass.

*We are a wound continuously healing.*

Listen to the beat of your heart
when you feel broken, it is
the most valuable and beautiful
piece of music still playing
in the orchestra of this world.

Storms exist
where our ghosts linger,
there is no rest
when we're haunted.

You've bandaged your wings
so many times before, they feel
the healing of heart and hands
before your human touch
graces their brokenness.

Oh beautiful soul
create worlds within yourself,
so that you can see
you were made for more
than this one.

*My soul is an ocean
filled with shipwrecks.*

Brave soul, I see you. Your eyes
tell me a story of a human trying.
Please continue, and I promise
one day you will see the beauty
this fight will carry you towards.

resi
lien
ce

*Fires of change forge
from the fists of women
who don't give in
and don't give up.*

Promise me you won't ever
lose your spark for those unwilling
to feel the warmth of your fire.

*I have ghosts to embrace,*
*they fear my strength—*
*this woman I've become.*

There she goes again—
straight for the fire
with clenched fists and
warrior eyes, determined
on surviving this hell.

Healing is a process
of picking up your pieces,
staring into each one and
whispering "you are worthy,
come back and make me
whole again."

*You are a soul bound together by strength, spine, and spirit.*

Feel the eruption,
let it flow through
your veins
fueling your body
towards freedom.

We are rising, and it is
breathtaking to witness
so many souls on fire
reclaiming their lives
from darkness.

I have been breaking
against the tides and
coming back to shore whole.

My wings are fearless tangles
woven together, making me
soar in a world forever
demanding that I fall.

*We are resilient as
the stars, and it is
beautiful how we
continue to shine
even in darkness.*

Your wings have a pulse
that keep you moving,
even when they seem
too broken to fly.

I have a tree for a spine
rooted in all the right places
to stand upright and weather
any storm blown my way.

Carve your name
on the peaks of your
conquered mountains—
let it forever be
a part of the battles
you have won.

Demons try to steal my voice
and silence my soul, but I
write words into waterfalls—
they all come spilling out and
I won't stop until it echoes
into every heart that has
endured this pain.

*I am a girl full of
riot and resolve, running
head first into storms—
conquering all that has
tried to silence me.*

We open up and bloom
so we can heal.
We heal so others know
they can too.

There is something
hauntingly beautiful in knowing
the world tried to break her,
but she got back up, rising
fearlessly with all her pieces
to mend more whole
than where she began.

*I am chaos and fierce
warrior,
steel spine and madness
and everything else too
beautiful to name.*

I dare you to live life
bright and out loud.
Throw gas on the embers
of your soul, stoke your fire
and reach for what you love
with a raging intensity,
that absolutely nothing
and no one can stop
your wildfire.

We are the fists
that will not uncurl,
the voices
that will not be silenced,
the bodies
that will not be taken,
the spines
that will forever rise,
and we will never apologize
for how much space we take,
for that space is ours
and we are worthy to exist
with a pulse and a name.

# *acknowledgements*

A special thank you to the team at the Self Publishing Agency—to Megan who helped me get this dream started, Ira who was the incredible project manager, Kelsey who spent time with the first round of edits and various other areas, and Laura who designed the inside of the book as well as the beautiful cover! Thank you so much for your patience with me, there are no words to express my gratitude for all of your time and help to make this the book I had always dreamed of.

To my Mom and Dad—thank you for always being there and showing me what it is to live life with kindness and compassion, and to my siblings; Jeanette, Craig, Jessica and Chad—you guys are my rock.

To my niece and nephew—my 2 favorite people in this world, you inspire me to be a better person.

To Natalie and our editing and writing beach nights and my sister Jessica who spent countless hours helping with the last round of edits and her thoughts and input to make this book the way it is, I could not have done this without you!

To Amber and Shantelle—I cannot imagine navigating this life without you. You are the most genuine, kind-hearted, and hard-working people that I know, thank you forever and always for being there.

To Cindy and Michelle—thank you for all of the hugs, and your overall amazing hearts that helped guide me to where I am today.

To Lynette, Clarissa, Kelly, Paulina, Marione, Keely, Katie, Eva and all of my family and friends, thank you for your love, guidance and support throughout the years. I love you all.

To Nicole, Faye, Shawna, Angie, Alfa, Rachel, Eri, and all of you other beautiful souls in the online poetry and writing community who has inspired me, lifted me up when I needed it, given me advice, shared my words, and helped me along this journey. Thank you for your beautiful words, strength, and vulnerability that paved the way for the rest of us.

Also a big thank you to everyone who has read, and shared my writing. I hope my words found you when you needed them the most, and continue to give hope and comfort. Thank you so much for your support, and for being a part of my journey!

# *about the author*

Janine Tamis is a poet and writer in the Vancouver, B.C. area. She hopes her words resonate with, and inspire others to share their stories, and to show that there is power in vulnerability. When she is not writing, she's out running, hiking, travelling, and spending time with family and friends.